The Haunted Through Lounge and Recessed Dining Nook at Farndale Castle

A Comedy

David McGillivray and
Walter Zerlin Jnr

Samuel French – London
New York – Sydney – Toronto – Hollywood

THE HAUNTED THROUGH LOUNGE
AND RECESSED DINING NOOK
AT FARNDALE CASTLE

First produced at the Social Hall, Tintagel, on November 7th, 1983, with the following cast of characters:

Thelma (playing **June**)	Pam Scobie
Lottie (playing **Marty**)	Erika Poole
Mrs Reece (playing **Lady Madge Graves; Mrs Slaughter**)	Laura Cleverly
Felicity (playing **Crematia**)	Joanna Brookes
Jasmine (playing the **Old Yokel; Arnold Death; Dr Blood; Rev. Tombs**)	Barbara Peak
Producer	David McGillivray

Directed by David McGillivray
Designed by Walter Zerlin Jnr and Gerald Tagg

CHARACTERS

Mrs Reece: elegant, bossy, enterprising; 50s.
Thelma: quick-tempered prima donna; late 40s.
Felicity: nervous, well-meaning but incompetent actress; late 20s.
Lottie: homely, down-to-earth, with strong Austrian accent; elderly.
Jasmine: attractive, versatile, fraught; 30s.
Producer: harrassed; late 20s.

PROLOGUE

The composite set consists of a main area, which represents the through lounge at Farndale Castle, and an area DR, *which represents a car*

DL *in the main area is a painted grandfather clock. Above this is a curtained arch leading to the dining nook.* UL *is a painted bookcase disguising a "secret panel".* UC *is a painted fireplace and over it is a painted window showing a view of the countryside. To the* R *of this is a door leading to the cellar.* R *is a practical painting of* The Laughing Cavalier *with cut-out eyes. Set at right angles to this is a door flat, for the moment representing the front door but which will be pushed back later to become the hall door* DR. *A table* DR *bears a vase of flowers and candlestick telephone and another table* DL *a radio, cigarette box and matches. In the area* DR *is a car (two-dimensional) supposedly driving up to the front door of the Castle*

The audience enter the auditorium to find the Producer and his cast of ladies still rehearsing the end of Act II. Mrs Reece, Thelma and Lottie are by the cellar door; Jasmine is lying on the floor L

Thelma Don't go on. It's too horrible.
Producer Can't hear a word you're saying.
Thelma I'm saving my voice.
Producer That's the level I want.
Mrs Reece David, dear: we'll have to stop there. Look, there's people coming in.
Producer Carry on.

Lottie moves off L

Lottie, you're in this scene, aren't you?
Lottie I have my make-up to put on.
Producer No, we're finishing this scene first because I am not going on tonight with such a complete and utter shambles.
Mrs Reece But they'll see the ending.
Producer They're not looking at us, Phoebe. They're finding their seats. Now will you take it from your line, please.
Mrs Reece (*to the audience*) Don't look at this.
Thelma This is ridiculous.
Mrs Reece Quickly, dear. You see I never knew that Mabel had had an affair with Maurice ...

Jasmine moves off

Producer What are you doing, Jasmine?

Jasmine I thought the vicar might stagger out of the door.

Producer The vicar is dead.

Jasmine Yes, but it's really boring lying here all the time.

Producer Get back on the floor this instant.

Mrs Reece Oh, we can't go on, David. It really spoils the surprise if they know the vicar's dead.

Thelma I agree.

Producer Cut to the fight then. Get out of the door.

Thelma We know this.

Producer Go from your line "Marty, I can't look".

Thelma This is an insult to me as an actress.

Producer Get on with it.

Thelma Marty, I can't look.

Producer Can't hear you.

Thelma I'm not taking any more of this. I'm sorry.

Thelma exits L

Mrs Reece Thelma!

Mrs Reece follows her off

Thelma (*off*) How dare he treat me like some bloody beginner? I joined this Society before he was born.

Producer Will you get her back here, please? Before I walk out?

Lottie Do we stop now? I have no make-up on.

Producer We're finishing this scene. I'm not telling you again.

Mrs Reece enters

Mrs Reece Thelma's very upset, David.

Producer We're going from Marty's line "I can't see. All I know is that this is a classic struggle between good and evil".

Mrs Reece (*to the audience*) I'm awfully sorry. We won't be much longer.

Producer We'll be as long as it takes.

Thelma enters

Thelma If we carry on with this rehearsal, I won't be ready for curtain-up. I'm just telling you that for your own information.

Producer Know your lines, do you? Do you know when you move across to Lady Graves? Because I changed that.

Thelma I don't think you need worry on my account. You just scribble away in your little script.

Thelma exits

Jasmine Can I get up now?

Producer Clear the stage. I'm dealing with amateurs. I must keep reminding myself. Get the music on.

Jasmine Half an hour I've been lying there. I could have been feeding Laura.

Jasmine and the Producer exit

Mrs Reece (*to the audience*) Bit of a last-minute panic. I don't know where the time goes, do you? We've been here since ten o'clock this morning. Lottie, hadn't you better go and get made up?

Lottie is about to say something, but thinks better of it. She exits

Mrs Reece mingles with the audience, welcoming them and selling programmes. Sinister music is played. When the audience is seated, Mrs Reece mounts the stage

Good-evening, everyone. (*To a woman in the front row*) Oh, hello. Didn't see you there. Better? Are you better? No? Oh, it's come up again, has it? Have you got something to put on it? Oh, the green stuff, yes. My son-in-law's got some of that. Yes, it does, doesn't it? Especially in the warm weather. Talk to you later. (*To the audience*) Well, what a wonderful turn-out. I think you're the densest crowd we've had for weeks. But no long speeches from me tonight because it's been decided that in future announcements of Guild activities must be confined to the Newsletter. This was a resolution passed by the Committee. In their wisdom. I voted against it, but that's by the by. It only remains for me to welcome you to what I hope will be an enjoyable evening for us all. Thank you.

The Lights quickly fade to Black-out. Mrs Reece attempts to exit. There is the sound of her walking into a flat. The following dialogue in the Black-out is whispered and indistinct

Where's the door? Oh, heavens.
Producer (*off*) Lights.
Mrs Reece No, no, not yet.
Producer (*off*) Get off. We're starting.
Mrs Reece I can't see a thing.
Producer (*off*) Ssshh!
Thelma (*off*) Lottie!
Producer (*off*) And lights.
Thelma (*off*) Don't you dare touch those lights. Lottie isn't here.
Producer (*off*) Lottie!
Lottie (*off*) I am not yet ready.
Thelma (*off*) I knew this would happen.
Producer (*off*) Oh, this is my fault, is it?
Lottie (*off*) I cannot find my shoes.
Thelma (*off*) Well, I'm going on without you.
Lottie (*off*) Ach, mein Gott.

Tremendous crash as the bookcase flat falls down

Producer (*off*) What's happened?
Thelma (*off*) Why can't we have some light back here?
Mrs Reece It's like the Black Hole of Calcutta, David.
Producer (*off*) Can we start?
Felicity (*off*) The bookcase has fallen down.

Producer (*off*) Oh, God. Let me through. Where's the brace? Go round the other side.

The Producer enters

Jasmine (*off*) I haven't got time. All right! I'll do it.
Producer Get something to hold it in place. Anything.
Mrs Reece What?
Producer Sellotape.

Crash

Producer Ssshh!
Jasmine (*off*) Sorry.

Thelma enters

Thelma Are we doing this play or not?
Producer Will you keep her quiet?
Mrs Reece Thelma, dear, withdraw.

Jasmine enters R and walks into the table, knocking over the vase

Jasmine Sorry. Knocked something over.

The Lights snap on full revealing from Rto L: Thelma, her skirt round her waist, pulling her slip down; Jasmine crawling on the floor; Mrs Reece and the Producer struggling with the fallen flat; and Lottie entering L carrying one black plimsoll and one white. Everyone looks startled and dives out of sight

Producer (*off*) Go out there and say something.
Mrs Reece (*off*) I'm sorry, I haven't prepared anything.
Producer (*off*) Tell them about the Guild activities.
Mrs Reece (*off*) Not allowed, dear. Committee ruling.
Producer (*off*) I just need you to fill in a bit of time while I'm trying to rebuild this bloody set!
Mrs Reece (*off*) You should have thought of that.

Producer marches on R with notes

Producer I'll do it.

Mrs Reece appears behind him and snatches the notes out of his hand

Mrs Reece Thank you. (*She comes forward*)

The Producer puts the set back together

Well, apparently we have a few minutes in hand. (*To the Producer*) I believe you want me to read out these items of interest, do you? The ones I was forbidden to read out by the Committee. (*To the audience*) Our producer's too busy to discuss this mystifying anomaly. So let's begin by welcoming two new members to the Society. They're both in tonight's play and so welcome aboard firstly to my enchanting Austrian friend Mrs Grosskopf, who manages the Alt Vienna patisserie in Stapleton Street . . .

Lottie (*off*) Wo sind meine Halszuckerin? Ich habe Sie auf diesem Tisch gelegt. Jemand har Sie weggenommeh. Ich kann nicht auftreten ohne meine Zuckerln.

Mrs Reece Some of you may be able to hear her getting ready. She's such a card. And hello as well to Mrs Boniface, who may be new to the bright lights of the Dramatic Society, but of course she's no stranger to the Guild. I'm sure many of you will remember her spartan endurance at the Whitsuntide Fayre. Do you know she spent eight hours selling five p kisses in aid of One Au Pair Families? She didn't come out of that booth once, not even for a pot of gooseberry preserve. Well, Mrs Boniface is now the proud mother of twins. And I think one of the little tinkers is backstage somewhere. Laura. Have you heard her? Nothing the matter with her lungs, is there? Now news of our fund to restore St Paul's Cathedral. This month's contributions were as follows: Mrs Daventry, ten p. Lady Molesey the Right Honourable the Dowager Countess of Tonbridge and Southborough, five p. The Reverend Bernard Ollerenshaw, thrity-five pesetas. We've also received the very generous gift of ten partially-filled Green Shield Stamp Books. Thank you so much, Mrs Treves. Are these things still redeemable? No, I didn't think they were. Well, these gifts will be presented to the Dean of St Paul's next Monday so if you haven't signed the card can you see me afterwards? Thank you. Once again there'll be no meeting of the aerobic class next Thursday. Whoever borrowed the Jane Fonda record, could you please return it? Because this is really most distressing. And if I may put in a personal appeal now: would all those members wishing to do passe-partout please bring their own gummed paper in future? It's not very healthy to lick other people's, is it? No. Well, I'm sure you're getting absolutely knotted with anticipation so I won't keep you any longer. This gentleman in the front row: hello! This isn't likely to happen, but if the blood should splash over Mrs Loosely, could you keep a weather eye open for her? Because she might have one of her bouts. But it isn't likely to happen. Thank you.

Mrs Reece exits

The Lights fade to Black-out

ACT I

The same

A series of sound effects is heard one after the other: an owl hooting, a clap of thunder, a cat's miaow, a body falling into water, a ship's siren

The Lights come up on the car in the area. DR. *Thelma and Lottie are sitting behind it dressed as teenagers June and Marty. June has a ponytail, wears a coat over a flared skirt and petticoats, and has bobbysox and sneakers. Marty has a duffle-coat over an open-necked shirt and jeans; he also wears his odd-coloured plimsolls. They sit waiting for the effects to end. June looks behind the flats. Marty looks confused*

June Somebody turn it off!

The effects continue: an explosion, chickens clucking, a creaking door, SOS in morse, breaking glass, and a typewriter which cuts off abruptly. Diverted by this blunder, June forgets her first line. She reveals a piece of paper stuck to the inside of the windscreen and puts on a pair of spectacles

(*Reading*) Marty, let's think twice about what we're doing. Your parents are going to be worried sock. If we go home now we can pretend this never happened. What do you say, darling?

Marty opens his mouth to speak and is drowned out by the ear-splitting effect of a moving car. Marty looks around. June encourages him to put his hands on the wheel. The volume of the sound effect is reduced

Marty Too loud!
June Lottie . . .
Marty It goes right through my head.
June What do you say, darling?
Marty No deal, baby. Back there only is hypocrisy and deceit. We agreed we want none of that business, and I climb the ladder to your room, and we envelope together. So that is what we do . . . (*improvising*) . . . and now here we are, driving along and having a good time because life is . . .
June Shut *up*. Darling, you're right of course. Just having you beside me gives me the strength I need. Where are we?
Marty This blizzard is so thick I can hardly see my face in front of my hand. Get the map.
June I can't wait to put our names on that marriage certificate. Just think: soon I'll be Mrs Marty Mortimer. (*She gropes for the map*)
Marty Look, there is a street sign saying Homepride Crescent.
June What does it say?

Marty Of course I'm sure.

June cannot find the map and produces a copy of the TV Times

June Homepride Crescent? But that means we've gone miles out of our way.

Marty Ach, Val Doonican is on tonight?

June According to this *map* we're passing through a mysterious village called Little Sainsbury.

Marty You are mistaken, June. We are not passing through but grinding to a halt. (*He brakes the car by pulling on the steering wheel as if reining a horse. Eventually it comes away in his hands*)

June What's the matter?

Marty hands June the steering wheel

Marty There's something wrong with the car.

Car effect cuts off

June What a disagreeable place in which to be stranded. Marty, I'm frightened.

Marty Pull your body together. Someone comes.

June It might be a madman.

Marty He tries anything on with us, what do we do?

June Give him the old High School Shakedown.

Simultaneously, they slap their knees, clap, spit on their hands and then playfully biff each other's jaws

Marty⎫
June ⎭ (*together*) Hot dog!

Marty Excuse me, sir. Yes, you on the bicycle.

A bicycle bell, clattering and banging is heard behind the flats

Old Yokel (*off*) Damn and blast.

    Jasmine appears

    Can't get the bike on.

She is wearing a dressing-gown and has nappy pins in her mouth

    Didn't have time to change. I've only just got Laura off. Who am I?

June (*with irony*) The old yokel.

The Yokel turns quickly, fumbles about and faces the front again wearing a crêpe beard

Old Yokel Be you talking to Oi, young sir?

Marty We have down broken. Tell to me where we get help.

Old Yokel You won't get no help round these parts, beggin' your pardon. This has been a ghost village these past forty year, arrrrr.

June But is there nowhere we can stay the night?

Old Yokel Nowhere at all. 'Cepting of course the Castle.

Marty We stay there. Show us the way.

Old Yokel Take heed, I beg of 'ee. No-one goes up to the Castle after dark.

Marty Why not?

Old Yokel They do say as how screaming banshees roam the battlements, swinging the blood-soaked heads they've ripped from the bodies of the living.

Marty But that is superstitious nonsense. Where is this Castle?

Old Yokel First left past the all-night launderette.

The Old Yokel exits

Marty The old fellow tries only to frighten us. Well, here is the Castle. I wonder if anyone is home . . .?

June Not *yet*, Lottie.

Black-out. Sound of howling winds. A spot comes up on the door revealing June looking up at it. Marty is far L looking into wings

Marty Here is the Castle . . . Thelma?

June clears her throat. Marty scurries over to the door

Here is the Castle. The other castles look very similar. I wonder if anyone is home?

June There must be, darling. Look, the door's wide open.

The door is closed

Marty Strange. It is almost as if . . .

June What?

Marty They were expecting us. Gasp.

June Marty, what is it?

Marty I thought I saw something move inside.

June Where? Let me see. (*She struggles to open the door*) Ah! Yes, there's something over there by the fireplace. What is it?

Sound of chickens clucking

Marty Phew. It was only a cat. Let us go in.

More struggling. Marty and June then go round to the other side of the door and try to open it here. Black-out, during which the door flat is pushed back to form a line with The Laughing Cavalier *flat and the car is struck from the area* DR *and replaced with a desk, telephone and chair. The Lights come up on the main area revealing Marty and June pulling the hall door open*

They walk through and disappear into the wings

June (*off*) What a magnificent baronial hall . . .

June enters, followed by Marty. The potted plant outside the door is caught on his clothes and he brings it in with him unknowingly

What a magnificent baronial hall filled with priceless antiquities. Wouldn't you love to live in a place like this?

Marty Not if I had to clean it.

June (*seeing the plant*) Shrub.

Marty What?

June Shrub!

Marty (*shrugging*) Not if I had to clean it.

June I feel as though . . . you'll think this is silly . . . I feel as though I belong here. Hello!

Mrs Reece (*off; imitating an echo*) Hello . . . hello . . . hello . . .

June Is anybody there?

Mrs Reece (*off; imitating an echo*) Anybody there . . . an . . . atishoo . . . bless me . . . anybody there . . . anybody there . . .

June We seem to be completely alone.

Marty I think maybe we should leave quick. (*He and the plant cross* L *to June*) I have the sensation of something following me.

June Now who's being an old scaredy-cat? Come on, let's go exploring. (*She skips* L *to the arch*)

Simultaneously, Marty notices the plant and hurries off R *with it*

June waits by the arch. Finally there is a noise behind it

What was that noise?

She sees Marty is gone and follows him off R. *After a pause Felicity bursts through the curtained arch as Crematia, the black maid*

Crematia Aaaaaaaaaaa! (*She is surprised to find an empty stage*)

Crematia is then pushed forward by Marty and June, who also come through the curtained arch

June What was that noise?

Marty I did not hear anything.

June You must have done. It came from behind this curtain.

Marty I will investigate.

Crematia (*weakly*) Aaaaaaaaaaa.

June Who is it?

Crematia (*prompting Marty*) The maid.

Marty The maid.

June She looks terrified.

Crematia (*suddenly terrified; pointing at Marty*) The prophecy is fulfilled.

June Marty, why is she pointing at me?

Crematia (*pointing at June*) Leave this accursed place. Leave now before it's too late.

Marty But we come only for shelter. Why you want us to leave?

Crematia Because the dead walk there, evil reigns supreme, and the central heating's broken. (*She moans and wails*)

June Oh, come—don't be glum.

Everyone crosses to picture of The Laughing Cavalier

Crematia If you think I'm a crazy old woman, take a look at this picture.

June Why, Marty: it's me.

Crematia This portrait is a portrait of the mad Countess of High Wycombe's portrait, and she was murdered here a hundred years ago this very night a hundred years ago.

Thunder. The Lights flicker

June Marty, hold me.

Marty holds her sleeve

Crematia She vowed with her dying breath to return from the dead to seek vengeance for being buried alive in this cellar.

Marty So that is why it is so heavily bolted and padlocked.

Crematia This door has not been opened since eighteen eighty-four.

Immediately the cellar door opens and Jasmine appears carrying a feeding bottle

Jasmine Sorry.

Jasmine exits

June (*prompting Marty*) Do you want to try and start the *car*, darling?

Marty No, no. First it's the thunder.

Thunder. The Lights flicker

I will try and start the car.

June Don't do that whatever you do.

Crematia Go now while there's still time. If *she* finds you here the night of screaming terror will begin.

June She?

Crematia She who waits . . . above.

Thunder. Mrs Reece, as Lady Madge Graves, is heard off

Lady Graves (*off; singing*)
              "Come follow, follow, follow
              The merry, merry pipes of Pan,
              The magic reed that charms at need
              The hearts of maid and man . . ."

June That voice!

Crematia (*laughing sinisterly*) Lady Madge Graves.

Marty ⎫
June ⎭ (*imperfect unison*) Lady Madge Graves.

Crematia The woman who . . . (*She stops*)

Lady Graves is supposed to enter. She continues singing "The Pipes of Pan", but doesn't appear

Yes, the woman who . . .

Pause. The singing continues off

June That voice!

Crematia (*laughing sinisterly*) Lady Madge Graves.
Marty ⎫
June ⎭ (*together, as before*) Lady Madge Graves.
Crematia The woman who ...

The singing stops. Crematia laughs sinisterly

Marty ⎫   ⎧ Why have we stopped?
June ⎬ (*together*) ⎨ Lady Madge Graves.
Crematia ⎭   ⎩ The woman who ...

Mrs Reece enters through the arch as the mistress of the house, Lady Graves, but dressed as a nun

Lady Graves Didn't hear the cue.

She notices the others staring at her in astonishment

Is something wrong? (*She looks down at herself*) Oh, what *am* I thinking of?

Lady Graves exits

(*Off*) Come follow, follow, follow ... oh, Lord ... the merry, merry pipes ... hang on a jiffy ... can't get my arm in ... magic reed that charms at need ... tra-la-la-la-la ...
June We're not waiting here all night, *milady*.

Lady Graves enters, this time dressed correctly

Crematia The woman who.
Lady Graves I've told Sister Philomena she can't hold the Rosary Rally here. Why haven't you announced our guests, Crematia?
Crematia They were just leaving because the house is doomed and we've all got the curse.
Lady Graves Crematia has such a vivid imagination. (*She takes a cigarette, picks up a box of matches and opens it. It is upside down so all the matches fall on the floor. She replaces the cigarette*) How do you do. I am Lady Graves. Welcome to Farndale Castle.
Marty We are honoured, milady. This is Marty Mortimer and I am her fiancée June.
June Our car's broken down.
Lady Graves Then you must allow me to extend the hospitality of the Castle. Crematia, sprinkle a little carpet freshener round the guest rooms and take these cases ... up there.

She looks round the stage for the cases, as does Crematia. Marty and June look sheepish: they've forgotten to bring them on

Crematia As you wish, milady.

Lady Graves quick-thinkingly moves to the arch and lifts the curtain

Lady Graves Can you see them, dear? They're just behind this curtain.

Crematia hurries through the arch

Goodness me, they're jumbo-sized, aren't they? Were you going on your
hols?

June Actually we're secretly eloping.

Lady Graves Ah, young runaways. That means nobody knows you're here.

The hall door opens and two suitcases are gently slid on to the stage

Crematia, some more luggage has arrived. Crematia!

June (*grimly*) Why don't I save her the trouble? (*She takes the cases and
marches towards the arch*)

Lady Graves Tell me, Mr Mortimer: how old is your charming fiancée?

Marty Seventy.

June Seventeen!

June exits L with the cases

Marty Seventeen.

Lady Graves Seventeen. How interesting. And where were you driving on
this beastly night?

Marty (*he has forgotten*) C-Canterbury.

Lady Graves Torquay! Well, you're miles from there.

June enters L, followed by Crematia

June Yes, we really ought to telephone the hotel to say that we've been
delayed.

Lady Graves (*to Crematia*) Can I help you?

Crematia I thought you called.

Lady Graves Oh, yes ... cases, dear ...

Crematia exits L

It doesn't matter now.

June We ought to telephone!

Lady Graves Please feel free to use our instrument.

Crematia enters L with the cases

We don't need you, Crematia.

Crematia exits L without the cases

(*To Marty and June*) Do you have the number? (*Moving L, she falls over
the cases*) Crematia!

Crematia enters L and falls over the cases

Get rid of these things.

Crematia You told me to bring them in here.

Lady Graves Why would I say a thing like that?

Crematia How do I know?

*While they are arguing, June takes hold of the cases and, unbeknown to Lady
Graves, throws them out of the hall door*

Jasmine (*off*) Ow!

Lady Graves I'm not discussing this now. Please take the cases to the guest rooms.

Crematia What cases?

Lady Graves (*seeing that the cases have gone*) The ... ones behind the curtain.

Crematia angrily pulls the curtain this way and that, looking for the cases. Simultaneously, the hall door opens and the cases begin sliding into view again. June tries to close the door on them, but pressure is being exerted from the other side. There is a backwards and forwards struggle for some moments until finally June manages to slam the door

Marty The number of the hotel is in my address book.

Lady Graves Oh, good. Have you got it on you?

Marty No. It's in my case.

Lady Graves Crematia, bring Mr Mortimer's case back here, will you? (*To June*) My dear, I can't help feeling ...

Crematia I can't.

Lady Graves Pardon?

Crematia I haven't got it.

Lady Graves Of course you have.

Crematia I haven't. It ... fell out of the window.

The hall door opens and a case is slid on to the stage

Lady Graves Ah, yes. The guard dog must have retrieved it.

Marty collects the case

Marty (*peering out of the door*) Good boy. (*He opens the case and takes out an enormous volume*)

Crematia exits L

Lady Graves My dear, I can't help feeling that we've met before.

June No, I don't think so.

Lady Graves Was it in another life, I wonder, or a formation dancing team?

Marty Here is the book.

Lady Graves Jolly D. (*She takes his case*) Crematia, you may ... Felicity!

Crematia enters L

(*Thrusting the case at her*) You're never where you should be. Buck your ideas up. You may now remove this. (*To Marty and June*) I hope that after you've rested, you'll join me for ...

She breaks off as she hears Crematia sobbing loudly

Marty Ach, Felicity, no, no, no, no, you must not be upset. Come here, my little one. (*She goes to Crematia and puts her arms round her*)

Crematia (*crying*) I'm doing my best ... I just ... can't seem to get ... the cases ... in the right place.

Marty The cases, they do not matter. We will take the cases.

Lady Graves Yes, of course we will. I didn't mean ...

Marty She did not mean to shout at you.

Lady Graves No, that was frightful of me. Come and sit down.

They are both leading Crematia off L

Marty Lottie will take care of you. Yes, she will.

Marty, Lady Graves and Crematia exit

Dumbfounded, June sits on stage and waits

Lady Graves (*off*) There's nothing to worry about. It's just me being an old grouch.

Crematia (*off*) I'm sorry.

Marty (*off*) Now you will sit down here. And Lottie will dry your eyes, so.

Crematia (*off*) Thank you.

Marty (*off*) Now it is not so bad, ja?

Lady Graves (*off*) Here, give me your hand, dear.

Marty (*off*) I tell you what we do. We finish this silly old drama and then we have Schwarzwaldkirschetorte mit Sahne, ja?

Crematia (*off*) Ja.

Some more muttering then Crematia blows her nose

Marty enters L, his face and hands covered in Crematia's black make-up. Lady Graves follows him in, her hands also covered in the black make-up

Lady Graves (*to the audience*) Sorry about that. (*She wipes her forehead with her hand, leaving a great streak of black across it*) I hope that after you've rested, you'll join me for our weekly communion ... with ... the spirit world.

She slows her delivery as she realizes that June is jabbing her finger at something. It's the suitcase, which still hasn't been taken off

Crem ... no. Perhaps not. Marty, would you do the honours?

Marty I'm sorry?

Lady Graves Since Crematia is indisposed, perhaps you'd ...

She does a fluttery gesture in the general direction of the case. Marty imitates it

No, take it *away*.

Marty Ach, ja.

Lady Graves Good. I sense that you are no stranger to paranormal ...

She pauses as she notices Marty standing doing nothing

Now, dear.

Marty Now? Ach, jawohl.

Lady Graves I sense that you are no stranger to paranormal phenomena ... (*She pauses again*)

Marty has taken the vase of flowers off the table and is exiting L with it. Lady Graves hurries after him. Both women leave the stage. Lady Graves returns with the vase and replaces it on the table

Perhaps it was no mere coincidence that brought you to my door ...

Marty enters L, Blithely picks up the vase and moves off L again

Lady Graves apprehends him and tries to wrest it from his grasp. Marty won't let go. The situation is resolved by June, who pushes the two women apart and flings the vase of flowers to the floor

June There we are, that's settled that, hasn't it? Or am I interrupting you? I mean don't let me stop you if you'd like to take it off and bring it on again another half-dozen times. Because it's riveting stuff, you know: trying to predict the eventual location of a vase of flowers. Or perhaps *I* could take it off and bring it on again? Shall I do that? That'd add a touch of variety, wouldn't it? I mean I've got nothing to do. I'm just sitting here watching you two sodding about backwards and forwards as if time had no meaning. Or what about this for an even better idea? Let's have the suitcases on again. Nobody's brought on a suitcase for thirty seconds, have they? I'll bring a suitcase on here, and you can take it out there, and then we'll have the suitcases dangling from the bloody ceiling, shall we, because that's the only place they haven't been yet. You know I really don't understand why you didn't tell me this was a play about furniture removals because, if you had done, I'd have phoned up Pickfords and they could have come in and moved the whole set around and I could have gone home.

Long pause

Lady Graves What was that, dear? I wasn't listening.
Marty June is real tired, milady. I will just go to bed with her.
Lady Graves Until midnight then.

Lady Graves turns to exit L then, as an afterthought, picks up the case and takes it with her

Marty I tell you one thing, baby: that Lady Graves is a strange person.
June I wouldn't say that. But she's certainly strange. And where have we heard that name before?
Marty Before I telephone to the hotel I speak with my friend Scoop Dixon.
June Ah, yes, the widely-read investigative journalist. He's sure to know her.

She finds a hula-hoop and begins twirling it round her waist. It falls immediately to the floor. Marty goes to the candlestick telephone and dials. When he speaks he holds the candlestick to his ear and speaks into the earpiece. When he listens he holds a piece to each ear

Marty Hi there, Scoop. Here is Marty Mortimer. .... I'm doing just great, old buddy. But let us get down to brass screws. What can you tell me about Lady Madge Graves? ... Ja. ... What? ... Mein Gott. That is unbelievable and horrible. We deal here with a crazy monster. Goodbye.
June Well?
Marty He's never heard of her.

June makes a second unsuccessful attempt to keep the hula-hoop in motion

Say, you do that pretty good. (*He sits*)

June Oh, don't be silly, darling. I'm only a common or garden silver medallist. (*Meaningfully*) What did the hotel say?

Marty Did I do that?

June shakes her head

Ach. (*He rises and moves back to the telephone*) Before you go, Mr Scoop, you do me a favour: cancel the rooms we booked at the *Seaview Hotel* in . . .

June Tor . . .

Marty Torremolinos. (*He hangs up*) What's next? (*He sits*)

June Why are you pacing up and down so nervously, darling?

Marty We cannot stay here.

June But where could we go? (*She takes off her coat and hangs it on a non-existent hook. The coat falls to the ground. She is wearing a diamond necklace, which she displays*) You know, what that old yokel said: this is a ghost village. So even if we did find a *Holiday Inn*, it would probably be closed.

She moves to cellar door, putting on her spectacles to find a pre-arranged mark. The door opens behind her, pushing her forward. She moves L

Now Lady Graves really couldn't be nicer.

A hairy claw appears through the door and reaches for June's necklace. June watches it out of the corner of her eye

And to tell the truth I'm really looking forward to spending our first night alone together in a spooky old castle.

She pushes the door shut and moves C to meet Marty. The claw is trapped by the door and wriggles frantically to free itself

Marty I did not know you were such a silly little romantic.

June Well, there: my secret's out. I'm just a starry-eyed fool blinking through my rose-coloured glasses. And you know who's to blame, don't you?

The claw disappears and the door closes momentarily only to swing open again. June goes to shut it. It opens and June shuts it. This process continues during the following dialogue

Marty Anyone I know?

June Yes, he's a Technical College sports champ, and all-round dreamy human being who made me fall in love with him.

June moves to the DR table. Marty helps her to place it in front of cellar door during the following

Marty Well, he must be one lucky son of a rifle to have found the only angel heaven ever sent to Guildford.

June Oh, Marty, I'm so blissfully happy.

Marty That counts for me double, sweetheart.

They return c

June Will it always be like this?
Marty Let us make a vow.

Simultaneously they slap their knees, clap, spit on their hands and then playfully biff each other's jaws

Marty ⎫ (*together*) Hot dog! (*They go into an uncomfortable clinch*)
June ⎭

June Oh, Marty, I'm so in love I think I'll burst.

Jasmine enters L as Arnold Death, a solicitor

Death What's this deafening racket?

June shakes her head at him

Death exits

Marty I love you also.
June How much?
Marty Too much to let you risk your life in this sinister place. We will listen to the weather forecast and if there is soon to be no more snow I will the car repair. (*He moves to the radio*)
Mrs Reece (*off*) Tonight all listeners are advised to stay indoors . . .
Marty Here is the radio. I switch it on. (*He does so*)

Pause

Mrs Reece (*off*) Tonight all listeners are advised to stay indoors. The howling blizzards will continue until dawn and they will be accompanied by sub-zero temperatures and snow drifts of up to twenty feet deep. That settles it, Marty. We're trapped . . . oh, no. That's not me.
June That settles it, Marty. We're trapped.

They move away from the radio

Mrs Reece (*off*) And now here is a newsflash. The lunatic asylum just down the road has reported the escape of Mad Slasher Daniels, the homicidal maniac.
June Marty, what did she say?
Marty Something about a homosexual maniac.

They return to the radio, listening closely. Fiddling with the tuner, Marty pulls the radio off the table and it falls apart, revealing itself as six pieces of hardboard tacked loosely together. Marty tries without luck to reassemble it

Mrs Reece (*off*) Mr Daniels, who has long, pointed teeth and hands like claws, is seven feet tall and covered in hair. He will almost certainly kill anyone he meets and rip them to pieces so lock all your doors and windows. One of the doctors at the asylum said tonight that Mr Daniels has already killed a hundred and fifteen people and left a further twenty-three half-mad with fear.
June It's too horrible. Find another station.

Marty attempts to find the tuner. "Rock Around The Clock" is heard. Marty and June quickly start jiving

Death enters L. *He also has black smudges over his face and hands*

Death What's this deafening racket?

He shuffles the pieces of the radio and the music stops

Marty We are just high-spirited and did not mean to disturb you, Mr——
Death Death. Arnold Death. I'm a solicitor and amateur beautician who has lived at the Castle for many years, and I was trying to wax my legs.
Marty I am June and this is my fiancée Marty Mortimer.
June How do you do, Mr Death.
Death Where did you get that necklace?
June Why, I've always had it. I'm told it was clutched in my hand when I arrived at the orphanage.
Death The orphanage? You mean you're an orphan?
Marty Let me put it this way, Mr Death: June has no mother or father.
June I like to think it was my mother who gave me this. Look, it bears a strange inscription I've never been able to decipher.
Death I know. I mean ... I know that necklaces of that type often bear indecipherable inscriptions. I say, I'd like to talk more about this. Why don't we meet in my beauty salon at the end of the corridor?
June OK.

Marty and June skip out

Death moves to the telephone and dials

The Lights come up on the area DR *revealing Mrs Reece, as Mrs Slaughter, holding a telephone receiver*

Death Hello?
Mrs Slaughter Hello, Mrs Slaughter, Matron of the Sunnydale Orphanage, speaking.
Death Operator? Get me Mrs Slaughter, Matron of the Sunnydale Orphanage, and make it snappy.

Mrs Slaughter hangs up quickly then picks up the receiver again

Mrs Slaughter Hello?
Death What do you mean, you can't get through?

Mrs Slaughter hangs up again

This is an emergency. (*Pause*) Ah, Matron. This is Arnold Death at the Castle. I need some information about one of your girls.

Mrs Slaughter picks up the receiver

Mrs Slaughter Hello, Matron speaking.
Death She's an attractive little thing and her name's June.
Mrs Slaughter What's her name?
Death Yes, I'll wait while you look up the records.

Mrs Slaughter I'll have to look up the records. Can you wait?
Death Yes, I'm listening.

Mrs Slaughter looks around for a record book and finds that it hasn't been set. Seeing Marty's address book on the main area, she goes across and takes it

Mrs Slaughter Excuse me. (*She returns* R) I've found what you wanted.
Death Just what I suspected. Thank you, Matron. Goodbye.
Mrs Slaughter I haven't told you yet.

Black-out. Thunder

Death and Mrs Slaughter exit

The Lights come up on the area DR *revealing:*

Marty and June rushing to enter

June sits and examines the articles in a vanity case

Death enters the area DR

Death Ah, I see you've made yourselves at home in my little lair. This is where I study the English Legal System and the problems caused by tired skin.
Marty Is it true that a face mask is designed to tighten the pores?
Death It certainly is, Marty. And of course it also cleanses them of grime and excess oil.
Marty Ach, good. Then I have won the bet I made with the barman of the *Rose and Crown.*
Death You may like to remind him that he can preserve the water balance of his skin by the use of a night cream. Try this one.
Marty Danke schön.
Death And what about you, June? Have you developed a skin care routine suited to your complexion?
June I do my best, Mr Death, but in all honesty I'm an absolute martyr to an over-sensitive epidermis.
Death Cleansing is the answer. (*He begins cleansing June's face*) June, listen to me. We haven't got much time. I have reason to believe that it *was* your mother who gave you that necklace.
June I don't understand. What do you know about my mother?
Death Ssshh. Walls have ears. Marty, you and your barman friend may be interested in this: when using a lotion cleanser, wipe it off first with a clean, damp cotton wool ball and then with a tissue to be on the safe side.
Marty I hear there is a strong lobby against the use of baby oil around the eyes.
Death Yes, I was only discussing this the other day during an application for an affiliation order. I phoned the orphanage, June. I know who your mother is.
June Tell me.
Death It's someone I know very well.
June Who?
Death Ssshh. Danger all around. For a sensitive skin like yours it's a good

idea to use an alcohol-free toner like this one. Whatever I tell you must go no further. If Lady Graves finds out I've been talking to you, none of us will be safe.

June You're frightening me to death, Mr Death.

Death begins applying moisturising cream to June's face and spectacles

Death Finally, moisturising is the most important part of any beauty routine. Used twice a day after cleansing and toning, it gives Mother Nature a helping hand to combat excessive water loss, and keep the epidermis smooth and supple.

June But I must know the circumstances of my birth.

A gong is heard off

Death Can't talk now. Crematia's serving drinks. It'd be suspicious if we weren't there. Time to present our fresh face to the world!

He is cleansing off the moisturiser with tissues when a baby is heard crying, off

Oh God, Laura's woken up.

Death dashes off

June is left spitting out moisturiser and tissues

Marty (*to June*) Is this the face that launched a thousand ships?

Black-out. Thunder

Marty and June exit

The Lights come up to half on the main area

Crematia, her black make-up now extremely streaky, enters L with a tray containing champagne and glasses. She crosses to the painting

Crematia Countess, it is I, Crematia, thy faithful servant. Speak to me, O evil one. Have I interpreted the portents correctly? Wilt thou wreak thy ghastly vengeance before the Late Film?

The eyes in the portrait light up (Stage Management shining two torches). Crematia screams. The Lights come up to full revealing:

Mary, June and Death all clustered in the archway waiting to come on. They all begin laughing merrily and move C

Death Well, Crematia, old girl, what's up with you? You look as though you've seen a ghost.

Crematia Tonight is the night of retribution. The Countess has spoken.

Death Don't give me that rot. The Countess has been dead for a hundred years.

Crematia Not dead. Only waiting.

Thunder. The Lights flicker. Crematia hands the glasses round

Her ladyship presents her compliments and hopes you will enjoy this bottle of Château de la ... something French.

June Champagne? How exciting.

Crematia For one of you it will be the last drink you will ever taste. Ha-ha-ha.

Death Well, hark at Miss Morbid.

Crematia begins to take out the champagne cork. Marty, June and Death put their fingers in their ears in anticipation. Crematia merely lifts off the cork

Marty
June } *(together, feebly)* Oooooooooohh.
Death

They move their glasses around trying to catch non-existent spray of champagne. This makes it rather difficult for Crematia to fill them

Marty Won't you join us, Crematia?

Crematia No. It is the drink of the damned.

Marty Well, cheers.

June To us.

Crematia Bottoms up.

The four immediately separate, Crematia and Marty moving R, *June and Death moving* L

Death June, come over here.

June What is it, Mr Death?

Death It's time I came clean. I don't care what happens to me any more. I've kept this horrible secret to myself for too long.

June It's about my mother.

Death Yes. (*He moves to the secret panel*) This may come as a shock to you, June, but you ought to know that your mother is in fact . . . none other than . . . this is who your mother is . . . it's . . .

He blathers on while glancing behind at the secret panel. It begins juddering, which shakes the entire set, but nothing opens. Death kicks it and it swings open slightly. After more shaking and scraping, the claw reaches out of the panel, feeling around. Death puts his throat in its path. Gripped by the claw, Death tries to heave himself through the panel, but can't fit through the gap. There is a tremendous struggle with Death trying to squeeze out this way and that. June, Marty and Crematia keep looking round, but have to turn quickly back to the audience when they see that Death still hasn't disappeared

At long last Death vanishes from view

June Well? Go on, I'm listening.

She turns to the panel and registers shock

Mr Death? Where are you?

Marty June, what's the matter?

June Did Mr Death leave the room?

Marty I don't know. I thought he was talking to you.

June He was. But he just disappeared. Mr Death!

From behind the flats Mrs Reece is making desperate attempts to close the secret panel

Marty (*to Crematia*) Do you know where he is?
Crematia Yes.
Marty Where?
Crematia He's dead.
June What do you mean?
Crematia The Countess has claimed her first victim.
June It's not possible.
Crematia (*moaning*) Who will be next, O evil one? How many more must perish?
June Marty, she's frightening me.
Marty You say he just disappeared?

On "disappeared" he throws his arms open, forgetting that he has the champagne in his right hand. It goes straight into Crematia's face

June He was standing right there.
Marty There must be a secret panel. (*He moves to the panel*)
Crematia You are deluding yourselves.
Mrs Reece I can't get it closed.
Marty (*giggling at the sight of Mrs Reece*) Well, I cannot see anything. Maybe there is a hidden catch.
June I don't think you'll find one, Marty. Something tells me Crematia is right. Mr Death is dead. We'll never see him again.

The cellar door opens, knocking aside the table with a crash. Mr Death is there

Death Oh, I keep doing that.

Black-out. Music: "Hush, Hush, Hush, Here Comes The Bogeyman"

Everyone exits

The House Lights come up. During the interval a female member of the audience is chosen to take part in the Poetry Reading

ENTR'ACTE

The Lights come up on three chairs set C
Mrs Reece enters with her notes

Mrs Reece How lovely to see all these happy smiling faces. Welcome back, everyone. Now we're going to carry on with the play in just a moment, but before we do, it's my very pleasant duty to welcome here tonight two representatives from the National Townswomen's Guild Poetry Competition. It's lovely to have you with us Mrs Tinniswoode and Miss Bellefontaine, particularly as you had such a dreadful journey from [*inaccessible town*]. Can you imagine, ladies and gentlemen, two hundred and thirty-six miles by tandem. And the last thirty-six without saddles. Extraordinary. Anyway they're here for the election of this year's Townswoman Laureate, so without further ado let's hear the three finalists' poems. And the first will be read by our own Felicity Cheshire, who has entitled her work "I Must Go Down to the Kitchen Again".

Carrying a folder, Felicity enters wearing a strapless evening gown which draws particular attention to her black face and hands

She sits on the far R chair and reads her poem expressionlessly with her head buried in the folder

Felicity   I thought I heard a noise in the bright, yellow kitchen
And when I went to look I found
The dishwasher had broken down
And the sound
That had shattered the hour I meditate
Was the sound
Of a shattered plate.

I heard the noise of the jangle crunch
And reached for the dishwasher's threatening switch;
"Click", it went as if to say,
"You've spoiled my fun
But I have spoiled your lunch".

As I handled the cracked, clacking crockery
I became aware of its wistful fatigue;
It had served its purpose and now resigned itself
To the solemn bin, landing thud
On an unwanted record by The Human League.

Flip-flop my slippers slapped as I slopped in answer to the
        urgent bell,
And there was Mrs Van de Vere, her beetroot face impatient
As she let forth with a yell,
"Hello! I've simply heaps to tell".

She waddled swishing through the door which shut with
        reassuring "snick".
I followed her and soon she sat
And sniffed and tapped and sighed and coughed and scared the
        cat with playful kick
And shouted, "Goodness me,
How can you live without the sound
Of children laughing over toys?".
And I retorted, "On the contrary
My kitchen's full of noise".

In mid-yawn Mrs Reece pulls herself together

Mrs Reece And that was out first poem, a charming piece by Felicity. It's wonderful, isn't it, that something so beautiful can come from the tragedy of a broken dishwasher. And now for our second poem, which is also the work of a Farndale Avenue Guild member. Here, reading "Lines Written on the Occasion of the Birth of HRH Prince Rupert of Moldavia", is Thelma Greenwood.

Also carrying a folder, Thelma enters, elegantly attired, and sits on the middle chair

Thelma   Hello, Prince Rupert:
                I bring greetings to you
                From all in Farndale
                Avenue.

Mrs Reece Thank you, dear. And finally a poem which I know you're going to enjoy because it's going to be read for us by a member of the [*local*] Townswomen's Guild, and here she comes now, up on the stage, Mrs [*whoever*]. Come and join us, dear.

The audience member comes on stage and is invited by Mrs Reece to take the far L seat. Ad lib conversation about her experience as a poet and at public readings

What are you going to read for us?

Woman "Tupperware".

Mrs Reece We're all agog.

Woman   I wandered lonely as a cloud,
                That floats o'er Weston-super-Mare,
                When all at once I saw a crowd,
                A host of golden Tupperware;
                In texture smooth and colours pale,
                Slightly shop-soiled in a sale.

                Continuous as the stars that shine
                And twinkle on the streets and parks
                They stretched in never ending line
                Along the shelf at Marks and Sparks.
                At least a thousand did I see,
                And all reduced to fifty p.

                Now oft when on my couch I lie,
                In vacant or in pensive mood,
                I'm glad I had the sense to buy
                These strong containers for my food;
                Glass may break and bags may tear,
                But you can't damage Tupperware.

Mrs Reece is dabbing at her eyes with a hankie

Mrs Reece Well, that was our last poem of the evening ... (*she sobs*) You must forgive me. I did find that a profoundly moving experience.

Felicity is also crying

Yes, I think we all did, didn't we? Thank you for allowing us to share that very special moment together. Now it's time to choose the recipient of this year's honours, and as always the winner will be the lady who draws the loudest response from the assembly. So firstly may we have your appreciation for Finalist Number One, Felicity Cheshire. Finalist Number Two, Thelma Greenwood. And Finalist Number Three [*whoever*]. I'm overwhelmed. There's absolutely no doubt about the winner.

Accordingly, Thelma and Felicity exit

The Townswoman Laureate of nineteen eighty-five is [*whoever*]—a worthy victor.

Fanfare

Jasmine enters with a cushion bearing a laurel wreath and a book containing the collected works of a well-known poet

Mrs Reece places the wreath on the winner's head

Here's your crown of office. And something which I know is going to be very dear to your heart: "The Collected Works of [*whoever*]". Many congratulations.

Jasmine exits

The winner returns to her seat

What an enriching experience that was. (*Referring to winner's laurel wreath*) No, don't take it off, dear. You've got to wear it for the whole year. Don't worry, it won't rot. (*To the audience*) And so to part two of our mystery play. It's not becoming too unbearably tense, is it? No? Oh, that's all right then. It's just that during the interval I thought I overheard somebody say they couldn't stand much more. (*To a woman in front row*) See you afterwards.

The Lights fade to Black-out. The three chairs are struck

ACT II

The main area now represents June's bedroom at the Castle. The flats are now covered by curtains with the exception of the fireplace; the cellar-door (now the door leading to the balcony); and the door DR. *Far* L *is a four-poster bed arranged so that access to the back of the bed is available through the curtains of the arch. The bedspread is covered with black handmarks*

The Lights fade up on the main area

Crematia enters DR

Crematia This way, if you please.

Marty and June enter DR *in awe*

I've made up this bed for you, Miss June. (*Patting the bed, she knocks the canopy down and struggles to replace it*)
June What a superbly grandiose bedroom with its ornate ceiling and rich, hanging brocades.
Crematia Not very many people have died in here.
June Where does this lead?
Crematia The balcony. But it's always kept locked in winter.

The door opens. June slams it

(*Hysterically*) Acknowledge the supremacy of the evil one, I beg of ye. Cover thyselves in pig's blood and light fifty black candles and she may spare thy worthless lives.
June That will be all, Crematia.
Crematia (*normally*) Very good, Miss June.

Crematia exits R

Marty June, this is madness. Why have you decided to stay?
June Because Mr Death mysteriously disappeared just as he was about to give me some crucial gen about Mummy. I must find out what it was.

Very loud and prolonged smashing of glass, off

What was that?
Marty What was what?
June It sounded like glass smashing. Yes, look! The window is broken.
Marty Gee, someone has a brick thrown through.

He is searching for the brick when the DR *door opens and a brick is tossed in*

Here is a message attached to it.

There is no message

June What does it say?

Marty (*trying to remember*) Er ... when the clock not striking but pushing makes ... in the night ... this is very good ... this clock here ... ding-dong ... I cannot remember the last piece.

June But that doesn't make sense.

Marty No.

June gasps. Marty, distracted, doesn't hear. June gasps again. No joy. She grabs his arm and gasps very loudly in his face

June, you remember something?

June This message and the inscription on my necklace—they're the same. I must tell Lady Graves.

Marty June, come away from that door.

June Marty, you're hurting me.

Marty You remember when I phone to Scoop Dixon?

June Yes. He said he'd never heard of our aristocratic hostess.

Marty I said that so you would not panic. What he actually said was, "Get out of there quick or Lady Graves will poison you and bury you in the cellar".

June Why would he say a peculiar thing like that?

Marty Because seventeen years ago Lady Graves was accused of murder. But there was no proof and so she leaves the court a loose woman.

June Marty, I'm frightened.

Marty Come on, baby. Let us show them we can take it.

June All right.

June slaps her knees, claps and spits on both hands. Simultaneously, Marty slaps his knees, claps and spits twice in June's face

You filthy beast.

Marty Now I will leave.

June Yes, get back to Vienna.

Marty What?

June I said I'm feeling much better.

Marty You want me, you call me. I will be upstairs.

June No, you won't, dear. You'll be next door, won't you?

Marty OK. I am moving to the house next door.

Marty exits R

June sits on the bed and brings the canopy down again. She replaces it, sits carefully and runs a comb through her wig, which comes off

Lady Graves enters DR

Lady Graves Is everything all right, my dear?

June Well, somebody's just thrown a brick through the window, and I'm a bit worried about the disappearance of Mr Death, the ghost of the mad

Countess, and the seven foot maniac with hands like claws, but apart
from that I feel really at home.

Lady Graves That's so gratifying. Now don't forget that somebody may
attack you with a hatchet. But don't worry. It's only the poltergeist and
he doesn't mean anything by it.

June You're so kind, Lady Graves. If I'd been lucky enough to have a
mother, I'd have liked her to be like you. *Don't touch the bed!*

Lady Graves The great gong will summon you to the seance. The blackest
hour of night will soon be upon us.

Immediately snap on moonlight

Oh.

Lady Graves exits DR

*June very carefully lies on the bed. After a pause, heavy, clumping footsteps
cross behind the set* R *to* L

June (*sitting up*) Shut up!

*The footsteps cease. June closes her eyes and snores. She stops snoring, opens
her eyes and looks around. She closes her eyes and begins snoring again. The
claw appears through the wrong gap in the curtains. The arm wearing it has a
handbag over the wrist. The claw feels around and then withdraws. After a
moment the claw (minus the handbag) reappears close to June's head. Briefly
another hand appears and adjusts the claw glove around the wrist. The other
hand withdraws. The claw feels June's face*

I can't breathe.

*The claw fumbles about, arriving on June's breast. June takes hold of the claw
and moves it up to her throat. With difficulty the claw takes hold of the
necklace and begins pulling. June chokes*

Stop it.

Mrs Reece (*off*) Can't get it off, dear.

June tries to unfasten the clasp as:

Marty runs in DR

Marty June, are you all right?

*He flicks a light switch. Full Lights come up. June sits up suddenly and the
claw disappears*

I was living in the house next door and I thought I heard you scream.

June Marty, it was horrible. A hairy claw came out of the wall and ... (*she
covers her necklace with her hands*) ... and stole my necklace.

*Marty tries to take her hand, but June whips it away again in order to keep the
necklace covered*

Marty It was only a bad dream, my little angel.

June It wasn't a dream. Look, my necklace is nowhere to be seen.

Lady Graves enters DR, *carrying the handbag and claw*

Lady Graves What's all this about a missing necklace?

June It's true, Lady Graves. It was taken by a sub-human claw.

Lady Graves That sounds highly unlikely. (*She notices she is carrying the claw, dabs her nose with it and then pops it into her bag*)

June (*calmly*) I'm not imagining things, I'm not. Don't you see? The escaped lunatic has broken into the house and soon we'll all be ripped to pieces.

Lady Graves Stop it, June. You're becoming hysterical.

June cries with no emotion whatever

June, control yourself.

June winces as Lady Graves moves to slap her face, but she receives only the slightest tap on the cheek. A second later a much louder slap is heard from the wings

I'm sorry, dear. I had to do that.

June stops crying instantly

No need to look so anxious, Mr Mortimer.

Not the slightest bit interested, Marty is picking fluff off his costume

June will be all right.

Marty I have never seen her in such distress. What can we do?

Lady Graves We're in luck. My old chum William Blood has just arrived for the seance, and he's a Harley Street neurologist. Willie, dear, could you pop in with your bag?

Jasmine enters DR *as Dr Blood with bag in one hand and baby over one shoulder*

What's this? A patient from the paediatric ward?

Dr Blood She's got wind. Now what seems to be the trouble?

Lady Graves This unfortunate waif seems to be suffering from hallucinations. Will you take care of her as you did the others?

Dr Blood You can rely on me.

Marty (*to the baby*) Who is my little princess? Who is my——?

Lady Graves pulls Marty off DR

Dr Blood Been overdoing things, have we?

He gets June to open his bag for him, then fumbles inside it with one hand

June, listen to me. We haven't got much time. I have reason to believe that strange forces are at work in this house.

June Do you know something about my mother?

Dr Blood Ssshh. Walls have ears. Just slip this under your tongue.

She pulls a baby's rattle from the bag and puts it in June's mouth

My guess is that you've seen people disappear without warning and misshapen hands stealing your jewellery. Am I correct?

June nods

Just as I thought. Well, your temperature's normal. I'll just take your pulse.

June holds out her hand. Dr Blood puts a cuddly toy in it and wraps a stethoscope round her arm

Don't be fooled into thinking that an escaped lunatic is responsible. I suspect the culprit is Lady Graves' long lost twin sister.

June Lady Graves has a sister?

Dr Blood Ssshh. Danger all around. Would you put out your tongue?

June puts out her tongue. Dr Blood hits her knee with a hammer

Say "ah".

June Ah.

Dr Blood Nothing wrong with your adenoids. I diagnose too many late nights, young lady. Take two of these after meals.

June takes a large glass bottle filled with Smarties out of the bag and hands it to Blood. He hands it back to her

Listen carefully. According to local gossip Mabel Graves died seventeen years ago when she was trampled underfoot in the rush for a home produce stall. But it's my belief she's alive and living in the cellar here at Farndale Castle.

June But how could I be involved in such a horrid story?

Lady Graves (*off*) Willie, come out of that boudoir.

Dr Blood Can't talk now. Madge wants me. It'd be suspicious if I stayed here. Try and get some rest. We'll meet again at the seance.

June See you later, alligator. (*She lies down on the bed and begins snoring*)

Dr Blood What a charming room this is. Oh, and I see you have a balcony. It doesn't look very safe, does it? I'll investigate. (*He "unlocks" and opens balcony door*) Just as I thought: this balcony is a death trap. I'd better go in before something awful happens. Oh no, my worst fears are confirmed. This ancient masonry is crumbling beneath me. What can I hang on to? Help! Help! (*With one hand he clings to the top of the door*) What luck. There's somebody up there above me crouched in the shadows. I say, you there! You with the deformed, claw-like hands! Can you pull me up? No, don't tread on my fingers. I'm falling! Aaaaaaaaaaa!

Dr Blood disappears off L, *then walks back* R *petting the baby*

June (*sitting up in bed*) I thought I heard something.

Black-out

June and Dr Blood exit

An owl hoots

SCENE 2

The same

The Lights come up revealing Lady Graves and Marty C

Lady Graves I've brought you into the through lounge, Mr Mortimer, because this is where our seance will be conducted. At this table Crematia will enter an unearthly trance . . . (*She pauses as she realizes the set has not been changed back*) How silly of me. We seem to have come into the wrong room.

They turn and look off R

The set hasn't been changed.

Quick Black-out. Mumbling. The Lights come up. Lady Graves and Marty are in roughly the same positions

No, this isn't the through lounge either. Where can it be?

Black-out. Mumbling. The Lights come up. Lady Graves and Marty look embarrassed. Black-out

The Producer and Crematia enter

During the Black-out the bed is struck

David, is somebody going to change this set, please?
Producer What do you think I'm trying to do? Help me with the bed.
Lady Graves But we can't blunder about in the dark. People will think something's gone wrong. It's no good. I can't get this to budge.
Producer It's caught in my trousers. Will you stop pushing?
Lady Graves The through lounge is just along here, Mr Mortimer. At the end of this long, badly-lit corridor. Marty, where are you?
Marty I am here. Where should I be?
Lady Graves Perhaps you can think of something to do while we wait.
Marty You want to see a card trick?
Lady Graves That wasn't what I had in mind.
Crematia Milady?
Lady Graves Yes?
Crematia I can play "The Harry Lime Theme" on my nose.
Lady Graves Goodness.
Crematia Would you like to hear it?
Lady Graves If you like.

The Producer exits

Crematia does an impression of a zither or similar vocal party piece. The Lights come up

Crematia hurries off R

Yes, Crematia's going to enter an unearthly trance and contact her Red Indian spirit guide Big Chief Running Water Softener. He's so helpful. We often use him to locate pieces of Tupperware that have vanished without trace, or, as we put it, gone over to the Other Draining Board.

Two chairs are passed through the arch L

Crematia enters R

Crematia The Reverend Tombs has arrived, milady.
Lady Graves Conduct him hither.

Crematia exits

A third chair is passed through the arch. Lady Graves sets them in a semi-circle L

(*To Marty*) What the vicar doesn't know about ectoplasm could be written on the back of a communion wafer.

There is a clattering outside the DR door. Crematia enters with difficulty, carrying a table and cloth covered with black handmarks. Handfuls of snow are thrown in after her

Crematia Step this way, Reverend. (*She places the table below the semi-circle of chairs*)

Another chair is pushed through the DR door by Jasmine, as the Reverend Tombs, who enters pulling a pram in behind her. Handfuls of snow are thrown in

Tombs Good-evening, Lady Graves. Tonight the ether is electric with the moans of tormented wraiths.
Lady Graves My feelings exactly.

Crematia adds the fourth chair to the semi-circle

Crematia, strike the great gong.
Crematia Take heed, milady. This heathen mass will summon the evil one in all her fury.
Lady Graves The die is cast. Fetch the girl.
Crematia Will you be wanting tea to follow?
Lady Graves Yes, and sponge fingers.
Crematia Very good, milady.

Crematia curtsies and exits L

Lady Graves and Marty follow her to the arch

Lady Graves I am in a reflective mood, Mr Mortimer. Will you play me something?

A three-dimensional piano painted on a piece of hardboard is pushed through the curtains of the arch

Marty What would you like to hear?

Immediately Tchaikovsky's 1st Piano Concerto is heard

Lady Graves I don't know. Something ominous.
Marty *Chu Chin Chow?*
Tombs How about *The Dancing Years?*
Marty I know. *Lilac Time.*
Lady Graves No, I have it. Tchaikovsky's First Piano Concerto.
Marty You mean this one? (*He mimes playing the keyboard*)
Lady Graves How beautiful. How tragic.

The music stops suddenly and the "piano" is removed. A gong is heard

Ah, here comes the embodiment of youthful poise and charm.

Much clattering and cursing as June enters through arch carrying another chair. She is now wearing an attractive party frock

And how pretty you look, my dear.

June does a twirl. There is another burst of Tchaikovsky. Everyone looks at Marty, who quickly mimes playing the piano. The music cuts off. June twirls again, but with less feeling

June I sewed the rhinestones on myself.

Everyone sits at the table, leaving the c *chair free*

Lady Graves Reverend, this is Mr Mortimer's fiancée June.
Tombs No.
Lady Graves What?
Tombs It's him first.
Lady Graves You've met him already.
Tombs No, I haven't. You left the line out.
Lady Graves Oh! Jog my memory.
Tombs Reverend, this is Mr Mortimer.
Lady Graves Reverend, this is Mr Mortimer. (*Prompting Tombs*) How do
   you do.
Tombs How do you do.
June (*prompting Lady Graves*) This is Mr Mortimer's fiancée June.
Lady Graves This is Mr Mortimer's fiancée Jean.
June June.
Lady Graves June, this is Mr Mortimer's fiancée.
Marty (*prompting Tombs*) You go "gasp".
Tombs Ahhhhh!
Lady Graves (*prompting June*) What is it?
June What is it?
Marty (*prompting Tombs*) It is almost as if.
Tombs It's almost as if . . .
June (*prompting Tombs*) No, it can't be.
Tombs No, it can't be.
Lady Graves Let's all sit down.
Marty That's it.

Everyone rises from her chair simultaneously and then sits again

Lady Graves Dr Blood has been called away to a neurologists' convention in Reykjavik. The seance may therefore commence. Crematia, bring forth your occult trappings.

Crematia enters L *laden with a table, telephone, radio, vase of flowers, etc., which she attempts to set*

Are they your instruments of necromancy, dear?
Crematia Of course not. But we haven't finished changing the set and——
Lady Graves Just do as you're told, Felicity.
Crematia All right! But don't expect me to *act*.

Crematia flounces off L

Marty Please, you will speak with kindness to Felicity.
Lady Graves I'm overwrought. I'm sorry.

Crematia enters L *with a rubber frog, a shrunken head, a doll with pins, etc. She flings them on the table and sits* C

Crematia (*flatly*) The spirits of hell draw near, and the doctor's dead as well.
Tombs I thought you said you weren't going to act? (*He picks up the voodoo doll and waves it into the pram*)
Lady Graves Quiet, everybody. Crematia's going into a trance. June, dear, turn the lights off.

June rises. The Lights instantly cross-fade from full cover to one central overhead green spot. June pelts across to the light switch, then returns to the table and sits. Everyone then realizes the table is not beneath the spot. Everyone shuffles C *on chairs, dragging the table until it is in the correct position*

Now whatever happens next, remember to keep calm.

Crematia begins moaning and swaying. She stiffens

Crematia The chief of the noble Indesit tribe is with us. Who seeks his help?
Tombs It is I, mighty warrior.
Crematia Speak.
Tombs I crave news of a dear, departed Tupperware lunchbox.
Crematia What colour?
Tombs Blue.

Pause

Crematia He's got one in yellow. He's waiting for some more to come in.
Tombs I'll try again next week.
Lady Graves Actually if the yellow's going spare, I'll take it. It'll go with the invalid feeding mug.
Crematia So be it.

Thunder

June Marty, what's that ghostly mist up there?
Marty It is Elastoplast.
June It's forming into something solid. It's coming towards us.

A Tupperware lunchbox is slowly lowered on to the table on a wire

Marty It's impossible.
June Marty, I'm frightened.
Lady Graves No need to get into a flap, dear.
Marty I will turn the lights on.

Marty rises and goes uncertainly to the light switch

All (*quietly*) One ... two ... three ...

On the count of three Marty turns the light switch, the thunder stops and full Lights snap on, and Tombs, Lady Graves and June all look away from the table simultaneously. The lunchbox is flown up, taking the tablecloth with it. Tombs, Lady Graves and June turn back to the table and look genuinely surprised to find it completely empty

June Why! It's vanished.
Marty It must have been a trick of the light.
Lady Graves It was no trick, Mr Mortimer. Believe me, that Tupperware came from another world.

During the ensuing dialogue, Crematia mimes very badly to the Producer's off-stage impression of a Red Indian

Producer (*off*) Silence!
June Who said that?
Tombs It was Crematia.
Marty She is still in a trance.
Tombs Let's listen to what she has to say.
Producer (*off*) I am Chief Running Water Softener. I have message for woman named June.
June Marty, that's me.
Lady Graves Crematia, stop this at once. You're upsetting the guests.
Tombs No, let her speak.
Producer (*off*) Tonight, June will meet Mother.
June My mother's coming here?
Producer (*off*) Mother already here in cellar. Mother is ...

Long pause

Lady Graves That's enough, Crematia.
Producer (*off*) Mother is Lady Graves' sister Mabel and ...

Long pause

Lady Graves I said that's enough. (*She shakes Crematia*)
Crematia ⎫ (*together*) Oh, where am I?
Producer ⎭
Tombs Why did you stop her, Lady Graves?

Lady Graves Because it's time for tea. Crematia, lapsang souchong with lemon, and serve it in the Wedgwood.
Crematia Yes, milady.

Crematia rises and mistakenly exits R

Lady Graves (*rising*) Well, shall we repair to the dining nook?
Marty Not so quick, Lady Graves. We have heard some damn strange accusations.
Lady Graves I would ask you to moderate your language, Mr Mortimer.

Crematia screams off

June That was Crematia.
Marty I go.
Lady Graves Stay where you are.

Crematia staggers in R

Marty What is it, Crematia?
Crematia We've run out of sponge fingers. (*She faints*)

Marty, June and Tombs rise

Lady Graves I'll take her to her room.
Marty I help.
Lady Graves No, no. I can manage.

She crosses to Crematia and tries unsuccessfully to lift her. Crematia has to heave herself to her feet while Lady Graves holds on to her. June waits for the pair to exit, but finally decides to come in with her next line. During ensuing dialogue, Lady Graves and Crematia travel across stage R *to* L *with Lady Graves supporting Crematia and holding one of her legs; she hops on the other. Their progress is impeded because Crematia insists on taking down the curtains she passes*

June I'm sure Lady Graves is up to something.
Tombs June, listen to me. We haven't got much time. I have reason to believe that, before her mysterious disappearance, Mabel Graves had an illegitimate daughter who has never been traced.
June Marty, are you thinking what I'm thinking?
Marty I sure am, baby. Reverend, do you suggest that my fiancée is the heiress to Farndale Castle?
Tombs Ssshh. Walls have ears. I don't know about you, Mr Mortimer, but I could certainly use that cup of tea.
Marty I will put the kettle on.
June Lemon for me, darling.
Marty Reverend?
Tombs Dash of milk and two sweeteners, please, darling.
Marty I bring crispbread also.

Before exiting L, *Marty is encouraged by Crematia to take down the curtain over the grandfather clock*

Tombs Arnold Death, the solicitor and amateur beautician, discovered that the missing heiress has only one form of identification.

June What is it?

Tombs A necklace given to her before she was taken to the Sunnydale Orphanage.

June But I was given a necklace.

Tombs Ssshh. Danger all around. Come along, Marty. What's happened to that tea?

Hearing this, Marty has time only to pop out L, dispose of the curtain, and re-enter

Marty Bad news, Reverend. Lady Graves has disappeared.

Lady Graves and Crematia frantically scurry off L

And all the doors and ... er ... glass things ...

June Windows?

Marty Windows, Ja. Everything is locked.

Tombs In that case our only hope of escape is through the secret panel that's supposed to exist in this room.

Marty I look for it already, but with no success.

Tombs Where's that necklace, June?

June It was stolen. This is just a replica Marty made out of milk bottle tops.

Tombs Blast. The necklace is said to bear an inscription which cryptically reveals how the panel can be opened.

June Then we're saved, for I think I can remember that inscription.

Tombs Hurrah.

June Now let me see, it goes after this fashion:
> "When old Grandpa's clock shows one,
> But does not strike the same,
> Push the part that shows the numbers
> And the maker's name."

Tombs Is that all?

June I'm afraid so.

Tombs I can't make head nor tail of it. You youngsters are supposed to be good at riddles, aren't you? How about trying to crack the code?

Marty Yes, come on, June. This could be a gas.

June Well ... "Old Grandpa's clock": that could be a grandfather clock, couldn't it?

Marty Yes, and "When old Grandpa's clock shows one" could mean one o'clock.

Tombs There's a grandfather clock there, and it's one o'clock. I wonder if that's significant?

June Shouldn't think so. Odd, isn't it, Marty, how we've never heard that clock strike?

Marty Hmmmmmm. "When Old Grandpa's clock shows one,/But does not strike the same ..."

June positions herself to pace thoughtfully towards the clock

June "Push the part that shows the numbers/And the maker's name". Oh! (*Inches from the clock, she trips stagily and manages to steady herself by putting one finger on the centre of the dial*)
Marty Are you all right, June?
June Yes, I just tripped on a loose floorboard.

Marty, June and Tombs turn to the secret panel and gasp, even though it hasn't moved. Tombs kicks it open

Marty, we've done it.
Tombs No. Stay back.
Marty Mr Death.
Tombs Don't look. It's not a pretty sight.

June cries

Tombs Yes, the game's over. I'm phoning the police. (*He moves to where the telephone used to be, and pauses*) I think I'll use the extension in the hall.

Reverend Tombs exits R

There are muffled voices off followed by a crash. Marty and June look unsure

June Speak to me, Reverend.
Marty It's no good, June. He is dead.

June screams

Tombs enters R *with the telephone*

Tombs Now for that phone call. Hello? Hello? Get me the police.

Gas comes out of the mouthpiece into his face

(*Choking*) Ah, deadly gas! (*He falls dead by the pram*)
June (*flatly*) Speak to me, Reverend.
Marty It is no good, June. He is dead.

June screams

June Take me away from all this.

Marty grabs June and drags her, protesting, through the secret panel. After a moment June reappears, followed by Marty

Marty I go first. Wait here.
June Hurry, darling, hurry.

Marty exits

June paces anxiously, kicking Tombs, who is surreptitiously rocking the pram. There is the sound of scratching behind the cellar door

Mummy! Is that you?

More scratching

Mrs Reece (*off*) Oh, spit. I've broken my nail.

June Don't worry, Mummy. I'll let you out.

She stands in front of the door. There is the sound of bolts being shot and chains rattling. June opens the door, closing it again when more chain rattling and key turning is heard. The sound effect stops. June opens the door. Sound effect of a creaking door. June has difficulty in synchronizing with the sound effect

Mummy? Where are you, Mummy? It's me, your little girl. I've come home. The kettle's on if you'd like a cup of tea. I'll come down for a chinwag, shall I?

June exits through the cellar door

The Lights fade to Black-out. There is the sound of dripping water

June enters and switches on a torch on the darkened stage

What a chillingly dank cellar with its slimy walls and thick cobwebs. It can't have seen a can of Pledge in ages. Mummy, don't the cleaners *ever* come down here?

Shining the torch round the stage, she illuminates Tombs making baby noises into the pram

Ah, what's that?

She realizes what it is and quickly moves the torch, picking out a black, stuffed cat. It is pulled across the stage on a wire by Felicity, who miaows

Oh, it's just a black cat. Well, that's lucky. But what's this? Why, it's an organ. It's the biggest one I've ever seen. It must have two hundred pipes at least. It looks as though it ought to be in a cathedral.

A tune is played on an electronic organ with percussion acompaniment

Who is that sitting at the keyboard?

The music stops

What are you doing? No, no, keep away from me. Aaaaaaaaaa! (*She switches off the torch*)

The Lights come up revealing Tombs still lying on the floor

June exits through the front door and then bursts in through the cellar door

Marty, wonderful news. Mummy's down here. She's developed these awful hairy claws, but apart from that she looks super, and she's wearing such a gorgeous Balmain original with matching accessories. When I first arrived, the poor dear borrowed my necklace to look at it, but now she's returned it to me. Marty, do come and meet her.

Thunder. The Lights fade to half. The portrait's eyes glow. June sees them and screams

Marty!

The portrait falls down revealing the Producer standing behind the flat shining two torches through. He freezes into a poor approximation of "The Laughing Cavalier"

There's something horrible looking at me.

The Producer ducks out of sight

The Lights return to full

Marty squeezes through the secret panel, followed by Lady Graves

Lady Graves Marty can't help you now, my pretty. Marty, can you help me, please?

Marty helps Lady Graves through the panel

Thank you. (*She holds a baby's feeding bottle to Marty's head*)

June Lady Graves, put that gun down.

Lady Graves Stay where you are. One false move and he gets it. (*She realizes her faux pas and puts the bottle into the pram, searching for a gun to replace it with*)

June Why are you doing this?

Lady Graves You might as well know the whole truth. (*To Marty*) Where's the gun?

During ensuing dialogue, Marty finds the gun for Lady Graves, then holds it at his own head until she relieves him of it

Just because my identical twin sister Mabel was half an hour older than me, this entire estate belonged to her. I suffered this injustice for as long as I could, but when she told me she was selling the Castle to an elastic factory, something snapped. I locked her in the cellar and kept her there for seventeen years.

June Go on. You must tell me everything.

Lady Graves No, I'm going to tell you everything.

She and Marty sidle towards the open cellar door

You see I never knew that Mabel had had an affair with Maurice, the earthily masculine gamekeeper, and that the fruit of their loins had been adapted . . . adopted. I never knew, that is, until tonight, when I recognized that necklace of yours. We tried to frighten you away, but it didn't work.

June What do you mean, "we"?

Lady Graves I was helped by Crematia, or, as she's better known, Loony Lena, the Stark Staring Mad Maid.

Marty Ach, mein Gott, what will become of us? We are so young and we have our lives to live ahead of one another . . . (*improvising*) . . . and I want to visit my grandchildren in Salzburg . . .

June Shut *up*.

Lady Graves You'll go the same way as the others who knew too much.

The hairy claw emerges from the cellar door and grabs Lady Graves round the throat. She removes it sharply

I'm speaking, David.

The claw becomes detached from the hand inside it. Lady Graves throws the claw over the flats

You will be reduced to bite-size pieces—courtesy of Robotchef. The church bazaar needs some more of my Cornish pasties, and I'm right out of mince.

She aims the gun and nods in the direction of the cellar. The claw returns, grabbing her and pulling her off. We hear the sounds of a struggle

(*Off*) Ah! Oh! No, Mabel! Take your hands off me! Ah! Oh! Stop it, David, that hurts!

Producer (*off*) Sorry.

Lady Graves (*off*) Look what you've done to my nylons.

June Marty, I can't look. What's happening?

Marty I cannot see. All I know is that this is a classic struggle between good and evil.

Prolonged sounds of struggle followed by silence

Now the victor approaches.

Mrs Reece emerges from cellar in torn clothing

June Mummy?

Mrs Reece It's all over, June.

June rushes to Mrs Reece for an uneasy embrace

Crematia enters L

Crematia Will our guests be remaining at the Castle, milady?

Mrs Reece Yes, Lena. (*Pause*) In the cellar.

Black-out. Music

CURTAIN

FURNITURE AND PROPERTY LIST

PROLOGUE

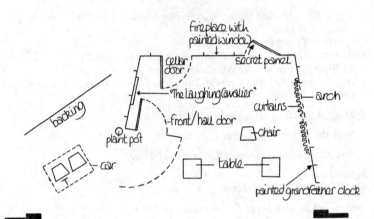

On stage: MAIN AREA
Table DR. *On it:* vase of flowers, candlestick telephone
Hula-hoop
Chair
Pot plant
Table DL. *On it:* radio (collapsible), cigarette box with cigarettes, box of
    matches set upside down
Curtains across arch (closed)

DR AREA
"Car" with detachable steering wheel
Copy of *TV Times*

Off stage: 1 black and 1 white plimsoll (**Lottie**)

Personal: **Mrs Reece**: programmes
    Producer: notes

ACT I

On stage: As before
Check front door closed

During Black-out on page 8

Strike: "Car", steering wheel, copy of *TV Times* from DR area

Set: DR AREA
Desk. *On it:* telephone, papers, vanity case containing cotton wool, tissues, cleansing lotion, toner, moisturising cream, pot of night cream
Chair

Re-set: Front/hall door flat to form straight line with R flat

Off stage: Feeding bottle **(Jasmine)**
2 suitcases **(Stage Management)**
Suitcase containing large volume **(Stage Management)**
Claw **(Stage Management)**
Two practical torches **(Stage Management)**
Tray containing bottle of champagne and 3 glasses **(Crematia)**

Personal: **June**: spectacles, diamond necklace
Jasmine: nappy pins, crêpe beard

ENTR'ACTE

On stage: 3 chairs C

Off stage: Cushion containing a laurel wreath and book of poems **(Jasmine)**

Personal: **Mrs Reece**: notes, handkerchief
Felicity: folder containing poem
Thelma: folder containing poem
Audience member: folder containing poem

ACT II

SCENE 1

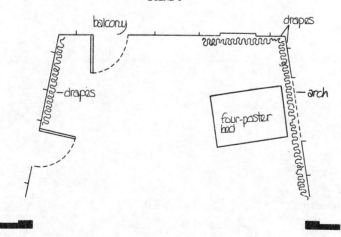

On stage: 4 poster bed with canopy. *On it:* bedspread covered with black handmarks
Drapes

Off stage: Brick **(Stage Management)**
Baby, bag containing baby's rattle, cuddly toy, stethoscope, hammer, large glass bottle filled with Smarties **(Dr Blood)**

Personal: **June**: comb, diamond necklace, spectacles
Mrs Reece: claw, handbag

SCENE 2

On stage: As Scene 1

During Black-out on page 31

Strike: 4 poster bed and canopy

Off stage: 2 chairs **(Stage Management)**
Chair **(Stage Management)**
Table and cloth covered with black handmarks **(Crematia)**
Snow **(Stage Management)**
Chair, pram containing gun **(Rev. Tombs)**
Piano painted on hardboard **(Stage Management)**
Chair **(June)**
Table containing candlestick telephone, radio, vase of flowers etc. **(Crematia)**
Rubber frog, shrunken head, doll with pins, etc. **(Crematia)**
Tupperware lunchbox **(Stage Management)**
Practical torch **(June)**
Black stuffed cat on a wire **(Felicity)**
2 practical torches **(Producer)**
Feeding bottle **(Lady Graves)**

LIGHTING PLOT

Property fittings required: nil

1 exterior, 2 interior settings

PROLOGUE

To open: House Lights on, full general lighting

ACT I

ENTR'ACTE

To open: Lighting on three chairs C

Cue 15   **Mrs Reece**: "See you afterwards."   (Page 25)
            Fade to Black-out

ACT II Scene 1

To open: Fade up to overall half lighting

Cue 16   **Lady Graves**: "... will soon be upon us."   (Page 28)
            Snap on moonlight

Cue 17   **Marty** flicks a light switch   (Page 28)
            Bring up lighting to full

Cue 18   **June**: "I thought I heard something."   (Page 30)
            Black-out

ACT II Scene 2

To open: Full general lighting

Cue 19   **Lady Graves**: "The set hasn't been changed."   (Page 31)
            Black-out, pause, then bring up full general lighting

Cue 20   **Lady Graves**: "Where can it be?"   (Page 31)
            Black-out, pause, then bring up full general lighting. Pause, then
            Black-out

Cue 21   **Crematia** does an impression of a zither or similar (Page 31)
            Bring up full general lighting

Cue 22   **June** rises   (Page 34)
            Cross-fade to green spot overhead C

Cue 23   **All**: "One ... two ... three ..."   (Page 35)
            Snap on full general lighting and cut spot

Cue 24   **June** exits through the cellar door   (Page 39)
            Fade to Black-out

Cue 25   **June** switches off the torch   (Page 39)
            Bring up full general lighting

Cue 26   **June**: 'Marty, do come and meet her." (*Thunder*)   (Page 39)
            Fade lighting to half

Cue 27   The **Producer** ducks out of sight   (Page 40)
            Bring up lighting to full

Cue 28   **Mrs Reece**: "In the cellar."   (Page 41)
            Black-out

EFFECTS PLOT

Please read the notice on page iv concerning the use of copyright material.

PROLOGUE

Cue 1	**Mrs Reece** mingles with the audience *Sinister music*	(Page 3)
Cue 2	**Mrs Reece** mounts the stage *Cut music*	(Page 3)
Cue 3	**Producer:** "Sellotape." *Crash*	(Page 4)

ACT I

Cue 4	To open Act *Series of effects as specified on page 6*	(Page 6)
Cue 5	**June:** "What do you say, darling?" *Loud noise of moving car, pause, then reduce volume*	(Page 6)
Cue 6	**Marty:** "There's something wrong with the car." *Cut car effect*	(Page 7)
Cue 7	**Marty:** "Yes, you on the bicycle." *Bicycle bell, clattering and banging*	(Page 7)
Cue 8	**June:** "Not *yet*, Lottie." (Black-out) *Sound of howling wind, cut after a few moments*	(Page 8)
Cue 9	**June:** "What is it?" *Chickens clucking*	(Page 8)
Cue 10	**Crematia:** "... a hundred years ago." *Thunder*	(Page 10)
Cue 11	**Marty:** "First it's the thunder." *Thunder*	(Page 10)
Cue 12	**Crematia:** "She who waits ... above." *Thunder*	(Page 10)
Cue 13	**Marty** attempts to find the tuner *"Rock Around The Clock" plays*	(Page 18)
Cue 14	**Death** shuffles the pieces of the radio *Cut music*	(Page 18)
Cue 15	**Mrs Slaughter:** "I haven't told you yet." (Black-out) *Thunder*	(Page 19)
Cue 16	**June:** "... circumstances of my birth." *Gong*	(Page 20)

Cue 17	**Death** cleanses off the moisturiser *Baby crying*	(Page 20)
Cue 18	**Marty**: "... launched a thousand ships?" (Black-out) *Thunder*	(Page 20)
Cue 19	**Crematia**: "Not dead. Only waiting." *Thunder*	(Page 20)
Cue 20	**Death**: "Oh, I keep doing that." (Black-out) *"Hush, Hush, Hush, Here Comes The Bogeyman" music*	(Page 22)

ENTR'ACTE

Cue 21	**Mrs Reece**: "... a worthy victor." *Fanfare*	(Page 25)

ACT II

Cue 22	**June**: "I must find out what it was." *Very loud, prolonged smashing of glass*	(Page 26)
Cue 23	**June** very carefully lies on the bed. Pause *Heavy, clumping footsteps from* R *to* L *behind set*	(Page 28)
Cue 24	**June**: "Shut up!" *Footsteps cease*	(Page 28)
Cue 25	**Lady Graves** taps **June** on the cheek. Quick pause *Sound of loud slap*	(Page 29)
Cue 26	**June** and **Dr Blood** exit *Owl hoots*	(Page 30)
Cue 27	**Marty**: "What would you like to hear?" *Tchaikovsky's* 1st Piano Concerto *plays*	(Page 33)
Cue 28	**Lady Graves**: "How beautiful. How tragic." *Cut music, sound of gong*	(Page 33)
Cue 29	**June** does a twirl *Short burst of Tchaikovsky's* 1st Piano Concerto	(Page 33)
Cue 30	**Crematia**: "So be it." *Thunder, continue*	(Page 34)
Cue 31	**All**: "One ... two ... three ..." *Cut thunder*	(Page 35)
Cue 32	Muffled voices are heard off *Crash*	(Page 38)
Cue 33	**Tombs**: "Get me the police." *Gas comes out of the telephone mouthpiece*	(Page 38)
Cue 34	**June** stands in front of the door *Sound of bolts being shot and chains rattling*	(Page 39)
Cue 35	**June** opens the door *Chains rattling, keys being turned in locks*	(Page 39)

Cue 36	**June** opens the door (2nd time) *Creaking door*	(Page 39)
Cue 37	The Lights fade to Black-out *Sound of dripping water*	(Page 39)
Cue 38	**June**: "... to be in a cathedral." *Electronic organ with percussion accompaniment plays tune*	(Page 39)
Cue 39	**June**: "... sitting at the keyboard?" *Music stops*	(Page 39)
Cue 40	**June**: "Marty, do come and meet her." *Thunder*	(Page 39)
Cue 41	**Lady Graves** is pulled off *Sounds of a struggle*	(Page 41)
Cue 42	**Marty**: "... classic struggle between good and evil." *Prolonged sounds of struggle*	(Page 41)
Cue 43	Black-out *Music*	(Page 41)

MADE AND PRINTED IN GREAT BRITAIN BY
LATIMER TREND & COMPANY LTD PLYMOUTH
MADE IN ENGLAND